There's A Dinosaur On My Paw

By Lloyd Lewis

Copyright ©2024 by Lloyd Lewis

All rights reserved.

No part of this book may be reproduced or used in any manner without the written permission of the copyright owner, except for the use of brief quotations in a book review.

This Book is dedicated to Fergus and Caewyn. They are always my inspiration to do better.

I was a pretty sad kitty today,
I couldn't go out and play,

I couldn't even reach the front door...
...because there was a DINOSAUR on my paw
(but don't worry, it wasn't sore).

I needed to free myself somehow,
so I unleashed a mighty "meow!".

Well that backfired, I won't do that anymore. The dinosaur replied with a big scary "Roar!!!"

I tried my very best to hide
but the dinosaur remained by my side.

One idea I had up my sleeve,
a boxing match to convince him to leave.

Unfortunately, that didn't go to plan,
I ended up with a 'hurty' hand.

Surely this dinosaur was breaking the law,
so it was off to jail, cuffed paw to paw.

The lockup plans soon fell apart,
so I tried to Wow him with my art.
But with my art I failed to impress
the Dino thought it was an awful mess.

So I thought I would read it a bedtime story,
about a famous cat and all it's glory.

However, the tale could not proceed,
I completely forgot that I could not read.

I switched to my favourite programme on TV,
that should have got it away from me.
The TV plan just went all wrong,
so I decided to treat it to a song.

It turns out that the dinosaur
was not a music lover,
I'm beginning to run out of ideas,
"oh brother!"

This part of the story might make you laugh,
I started to knit my friend a scarf.
I thought at least I might get a big cuddle
but all I got were my paws in a muddle.

I noticed the dinosaur was a bit of a cutey, so I tried to bring out its inner beauty.

The beauty thing just wasn't for me,
So I took dinosaur for a dip in the sea.

What was I doing? What was I thinking? I'd forgotten that water's only for drinking. But Cats and water just don't mix, what would get me out of this terrible fix?

I know, what might be super groovy,
let Disco-Dino have a bit of a boogie.

Disco music wasn't Dino's cup of tea,
So perhaps it would try some ballet with me.
(The ballet proved tutu much)

The dancing had made us hungry beasts,
Perhaps it was time for afternoon feasts.

How could my bottom have got it so wrong.
Sorry dear Dinosaur... for the terrible pong!

Once the air had cleared of the stinky menace, I said, "Oi Dino!, anyone for tennis?"

I've tried so many things to get this to end,
I only wanted to make it my friend.

When I finally sat down to have
a little think,
I remembered that dinosaurs are actually...
extinct!

In that moment I felt the Dino disappear,
I was now free to live a life without fear.

I decided to go and have a litttle snore and dream of dinosaurs, standing on my paw.

So sometimes problems can seem bigger than they first appear. Especially if we over think things.

It is important to take a moment and think through your problem. This can often help us see it for what it truly is.

The End

Sometimes we can make our own problems seem bigger than they actually are. It is important to think about them and try and see them for what they are. We can often shrink our dinosaur sized problems if we just take a moment to think about them calmly.

Printed in Great Britain
by Amazon